When God Was a Little Girl

A story about **God, creation,** and what it means to be **human.**

Written by
David R. Weiss

Illustrations by
Joan Hernandez Lindeman

Dedicated to my daughter Susanna, whose hunger for—and delight in—stories
has taken us to places both playful and sacred.

D.W.

Dedicated to my mother and father, who gave me the freedom to be a little girl.

J.H.L.

Book design and typesetting by Jenna Larson
Edited by Hanna Kjeldbjerg and Lily Coyle

ACTA Publications
4848 North Clark Street
Chicago, Illinois 60640
(800) 397-2282
www.actapublications.com

Library of Congress Control Number: 2013918169
ISBN: 978-0-87946-558-2
First Edition published by Beaver's Pond Press, Edina, Minnesota

Printed in the United States of America by Total Printing Systems
Year 25 24 23 22 21 20 19 18 17 16
Printing 15 14 13 12 11 10 9 8 7 6 5 4

"Tell me a story, Daddy . . ."

It's a long car ride from Madison, Wisconsin to Decorah, Iowa, and a good story always helped the miles fly by.

"What kind of a story?"

"Um . . . tell me a story . . . about when God was a little girl," she announced, her eyes twinkling with this divine little twist.

"Okay . . . when God was a little girl . . . she liked art projects."

"Art projects?!" Susanna echoed in delight from the backseat.

"Yes, art projects. She liked to do art projects just like you do. Which is a good thing, because that's how the world came to be."

"Really?"

"Really. Let me tell you about it."

"In the beginning there was only God. Nothing else was made yet."

"Daddy, wait . . . was God lonely?"

"Lonely? Let's see . . . when you're lonely do you smile and giggle?"

"No!"

"Well, then I don't think God was lonely, because already, before anything was made, she was giggling."

"Giggling?"

"Yep—giggling. Because she was imagining all the things she was going to make, and her imagination tickled her heart the way a feather tickles your ear."

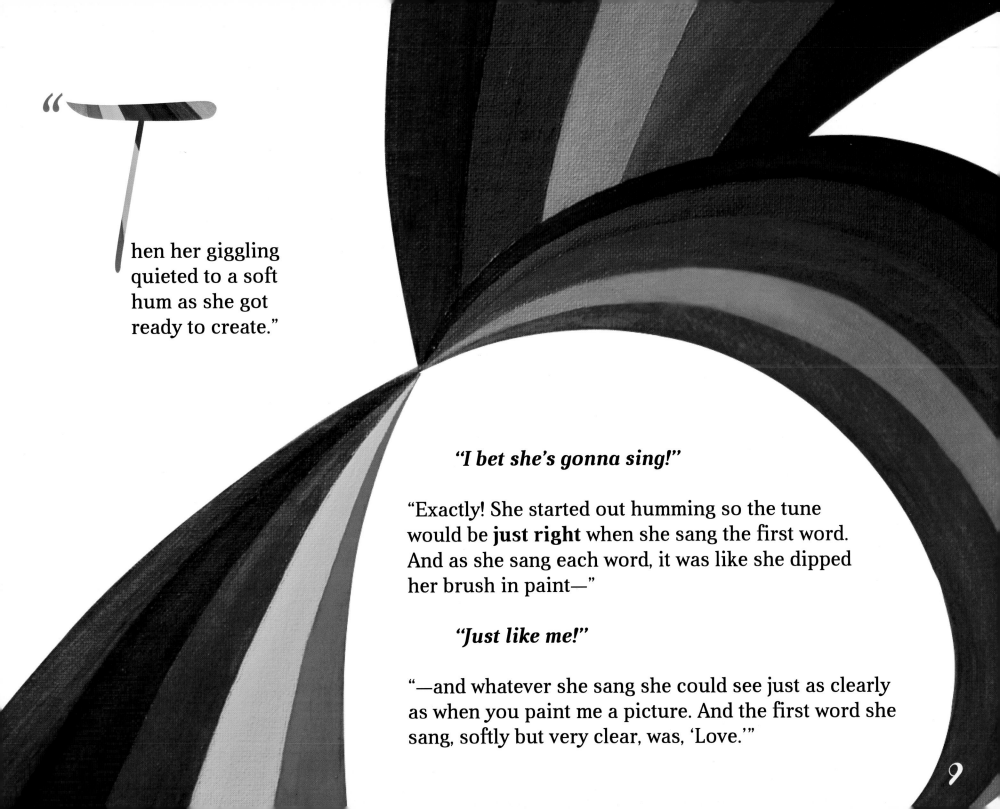

"Then her giggling quieted to a soft hum as she got ready to create."

"I bet she's gonna sing!"

"Exactly! She started out humming so the tune would be **just right** when she sang the first word. And as she sang each word, it was like she dipped her brush in paint—"

"Just like me!"

"—and whatever she sang she could see just as clearly as when you paint me a picture. And the first word she sang, softly but very clear, was, 'Love.'"

9

nd the Love looked like …"

"Mmm . . . darkness. It was all dark."

"Ah, midnight blue: the color of the sky in the middle of the night? The deepest blue you can imagine, even darker than black. Why do you think Love was that color?"

"Because, Daddy, that's just like Love. It's there, even when you can't see it. Love always finds you in the darkness, and when it holds you close, you know you're home."

"That's beautiful, darling. So, before anything else was made, there was Love. Love, like deep, dark blue, has always been here."

"Yup. Love was what God felt when she was giggling. And Love was the first color God painted when she sang."

ext, God sang so loud she almost startled herself: 'Light!' And bright yellow and white went splashing everywhere, like sunshine rushing through the windshield so bright you can hardly see."

"So bright that even God had to squint! So . . . she took a bunch of the light, rolled it into a ball, and threw it into the sky singing, 'Sun.'"

"Then she took another bunch of light and made another ball. And when she tossed this one into the sky she sang its name like the sound of a lullaby . . ."

"'Moon.'"

"And then, Susanna, God got out the glue."

"The glue?!"

"Yes. And the glitter. Because after the two big balls of light, mostly all that was left were little bits of shining light here and there. So God squeezed out some glue onto her paper—"

"Except her paper was the sky!"

"—and she tossed the glitter bits up until they stuck in twinkling patterns all across the sky."

"Stars!"

"Yes, and that's just how she sounded when she sang their name to them."

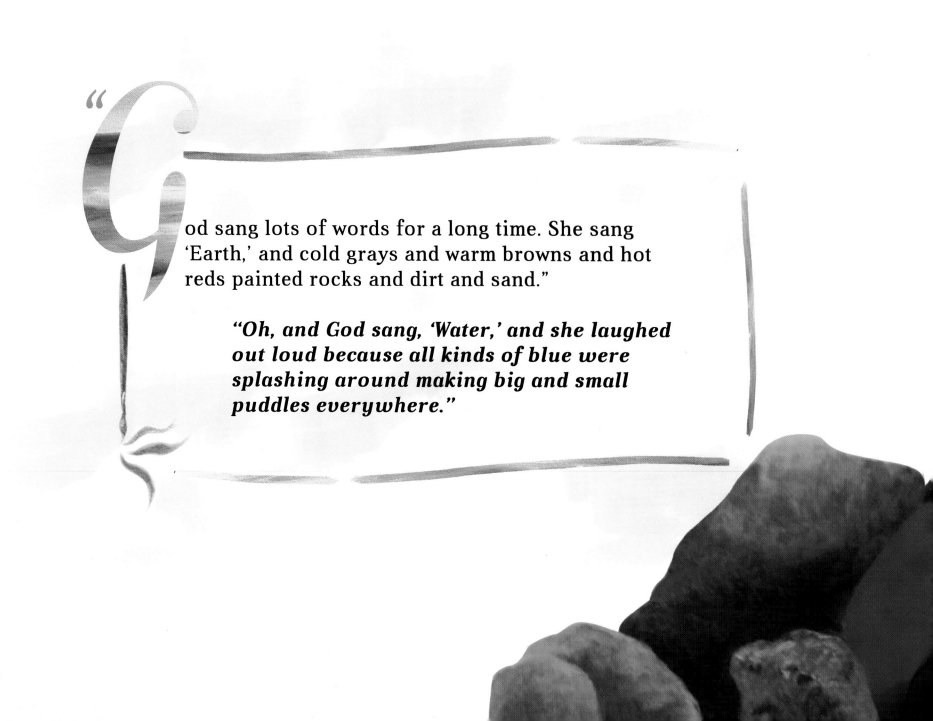

"God sang lots of words for a long time. She sang 'Earth,' and cold grays and warm browns and hot reds painted rocks and dirt and sand."

"Oh, and God sang, 'Water,' and she laughed out loud because all kinds of blue were splashing around making big and small puddles everywhere."

14

od sang 'Green'—"

"And the Earth and Water and Sun and Love, they all danced together while God sang—"

"And the Green was like the sunflower seeds and bean seeds you help me plant in the garden. God grew grass and bushes and trees and flowers of every color."

"God grew a great big Garden. Just like we do!"

"Just like we do. It was a very pretty picture God painted, don't you think?"

"Yes."

"What do you suppose she did next?"

"I don't know."

"Yes you do. What do you do when you make pictures?"

"I give them to you!"

"And that's just what God did. God made someone to share the picture with, someone who could giggle next to God at how pretty everything was."

"*W*ho?"

"Us. God took some Earth and made us. She found the softest, nicest-smelling Earth, the Earth that comes from plants when they turn back into dirt, and she called this Earth, 'Humus.' And she rolled the humus between her fingers just like when you play with clay."

"So then she smiled and giggled, and she made Humus Beings. Bunches of them!"

"And each one was a little different. Some were the color of deep, dark dirt; some looked like the pale sand on the beach."

"Some were boys and some were girls. Some were taller; some were shorter. Some were thin; some were round. And God thought they all looked just right!"

"And she sang to them that they were Human Beings."

"They all looked at the Garden and at each other, and they said, 'This is good!'"

"And you know what God said?"

**"W**hat?"

"God said, 'Thanks, but I'm not done singing yet.' And while the Human Beings watched wide-eyed, God sang—"

"I know!—and her song painted every type of Animal. Then she said with a big grin, 'You can't have a Party without lots of company!'"

"And she invited the Human Beings to help her, saying, 'Now it's your turn to sing. Your special job in the Garden is to be Echoes of me. I made the animals with my singing. You get to name them with your singing.'"

"And then God explained, 'This is how you become friends with everything in the Garden. See, it's a great big Song. When you name each Animal—and the Plants, too—you can hear how all the notes fit together.'"

"So all afternoon God listened while the Human Beings sang names to every Plant and Animal in the Garden and learned the great big Song that mixed all the notes together. It sounded like the rainbow."

"The rainbow?"

"The rainbow, Daddy. Because as they named each animal, the words fit together just like the colors in the rainbow: they made the whole picture look most beautiful."

"And as the Sun set, God yawned—like little girls do when they're tuckered out by big art projects—and she said, 'Let's all take a nap. We'll have the Party tomorrow.' And so they did."

(Triumphantly,) *"And that's what happened . . . when God was a little girl."*

"*Daddy . . . (big yawn) . . . did it really happen like that?*"

"Sure it did. It always happens just like the stories say . . . even when the stories tell it differently each time."

"*Daddy . . .*" came a sleepy voice from behind me, "*I love you.*"

"I love you, too, Susanna. I love you, too."

e pulled up to the house, and as I carried this sleeping bundle of trust inside I whispered in her ear, "And Susanna, when God was a little girl, that's what she said to each of us before the Party began. She said, 'I love you.'

"God made us to be little echoes of the giggles that she felt already before there was anything at all. And when we live as the Echo of God, we say 'I love you' right back to her, and to everything else, just like I did to you."

And from somewhere in her dreams a little voice smiled up to me, *"I know, Daddy. That's why I asked you to tell me a story."*

David Weiss – Trained as a theologian, David thinks about God … all the time. Whether as a father or grandfather, college instructor or Sunday School teacher, poet or writer, he seeks to imagine God in ways that are helpful and hopeful. In this book he brings insights from seminary and graduate school into a story that is deceptively simple and simply profound. David and his wife, Margaret, live in Saint Paul, Minnesota, where they have a blended family of five children and seven grandchildren (and probably more to come!). They like keeping close company with creation and have had dogs, cats, birds, fish, guinea pigs, hamsters, and even worms as pets. Their home, like their life, is fairly cluttered with joy.

Joan Hernandez Lindeman – Growing up on a dairy farm in southeastern Minnesota allowed Joan to develop a close bond with nature, the seasons, and God. Many of the paintings in this story were inspired by the beauty and strength in nature, and deepened by the joy of experiencing it as a child. Joan's involvement in intercultural learning, diverse communities, and urban school settings influences her racially diverse representations of God in this story. Today, Joan continues to commit her time to teaching, specializing in elementary reading instruction. Her passion is promoting equity in schools and helping all students succeed. Joan's family and great friends are her daily inspiration.

To learn more about the book and to find resources for using *When God Was a Little Girl* in classroom discussions with children or in adult forums visit:

www.WhenGodWasaLittleGirl.com